C R E A T I V E
ENTREPRENEURSHIP

CREATIVE ENTREPRENEURSHIP

"A BLUEPRINT FOR BUSINESS AND JOB CREATION AND ECONOMIC PROSPERITY IN THE COMMUNITY"

ABRAHAM JOSEPH

iUniverse, Inc.
Bloomington

CREATIVE ENTREPRENEURSHIP
"A BLUEPRINT FOR BUSINESS AND JOB CREATION AND ECONOMIC PROSPERITY IN THE COMMUNITY"

iUniverse books may be ordered through booksellers or by contacting:

iUniverse
1663 Liberty Drive
Bloomington, IN 47403
www.iuniverse.com
1-800-Authors (1-800-288-4677)

Because of the dynamic nature of the Internet, any web addresses or links contained in this book may have changed since publication and may no longer be valid. The views expressed in this work are solely those of the author and do not necessarily reflect the views of the publisher, and the publisher hereby disclaims any responsibility for them.

Any people depicted in stock imagery provided by Thinkstock are models, and such images are being used for illustrative purposes only.
Certain stock imagery © Thinkstock.

ISBN: 978-1-4620-4945-5 (sc)
ISBN: 978-1-4620-4946-2 (ebk)

Printed in the United States of America

iUniverse rev. date: 10/11/2011

ACKNOWLEDGMENTS

I dedicate this book to my father, Abe Joseph Sr.; my grandfather Joe H. Joseph; and my great-grandfather Jacob Joseph. Jacob Joseph was the patriarch of the Joseph family. Born in slavery in South Carolina, Jacob was later sold to a plantation owner and lived and worked in southeast Georgia and north Florida. He eventually purchased his freedom and married Isabella Dawson. They raised fourteen children (seven boys and seven girls). Jacob was a farmer and ran a business featuring a technology called the "dipping well." This dipping well was used to sanitize livestock by ridding them of fleas, ticks, and other parasites. Farmers from southeast Georgia and north Florida would bring their livestock to my great-grandfather for treatment.

Joe H. Joseph was Jacob's oldest son and my grandfather. Joe married Katie, and they also had fourteen children (seven boys and seven girls). My grandfather was also a farmer and sold his produce at market. In addition, he produced and sold turpentine. My father, Abe Joseph Sr., (known as Ham) married my mom, Maude, and they had eight children (five girls and three boys). My father, a World War II army veteran, worked for and retired from the local paper mill as a laborer, but he was also a farmer. My father grew various types of crops and raised hogs. He sold produce, meat, and homemade syrup to the public. My father also was known for his barbeque, which featured his famous sauce. He sold his barbeque to new and regular customers throughout southeast Georgia.

I also would like to acknowledge my mother's parents Hammond and Ada Roberts. During the early 1900s, my grandparents owned and operated a general store and post office in the Kinlaw Community of southeast Georgia.

As you can see, entrepreneurship is in my blood. All of this inspired me to own and operate an accounting, tax, and consulting business for over thirty-one years. I have also started and operated other business ventures.

My ultimate acknowledgement is to God, who has created opportunities for me and protected me throughout my life during the good and bad times.

I am excited about sharing my knowledge and experiences as well as the knowledge and experiences of other people. I hope you enjoy this book, and I wish you much success!

Jacob Joseph taking his produce to the market in the late 1800s.

A mirror image of Joe H. Joseph and Hammond Roberts in the early 1900s

CONTENTS

INTRODUCTION

The purpose of this book is to encourage and inspire all who seek to venture down the entrepreneurship road. I will share details of my own personal and professional experiences with operating businesses. The book also includes testimonies and experiences from other business owners regarding their successes and failures. The main goal of this book is to encourage a mindset of community growth through economic prosperity.

I applaud individuals who devote their time and money to realizing their dreams of owning and operating profitable businesses. Their devotion and commitment can result in self-respect, recognition, increased community spirit, and financial security for the entrepreneur and his or her loved ones.

In the pages ahead, I will identify the different types of business structures and encourage you to research the business you are interested in operating. The book will emphasize developing a good business plan, identifying sources of financing, establishing rapport with key people, properly managing your business, and establishing effective recordkeeping. Finally, I will conclude with an effective community economic model.

CHAPTER 1

The Different Types of Business Structures

The intent of this chapter is to give you a general knowledge of the different types of business structures. More detailed information can be obtained from accounting books, Internal Revenue Service (IRS) regulations, your professional accountant, and qualified lawyers and academics.

Normally, a potential business owner has five types of business structures to choose from: sole proprietorship, partnership, corporation, Subchapter S corporation, and limited liability corporation.

Sole Proprietorship

A sole proprietorship is owned by one individual. All liabilities and assets belong to this sole owner or proprietor. Profits from a sole proprietorship are passed on to the proprietor's personal income tax return and are subject to self-employment taxes. The self-employment tax maybe equal to twice the Social Security and Medicare tax rates.

A sole proprietorship offers the following advantages:

1. it is cheaper to start and discontinue, and
2. it allows for individual control and management.

The disadvantages of a sole proprietorship include the following:

1. self employment taxes,
2. the need to raise capital, and
3. unlimited liability.

Unlimited liability means that if there are debts, liens, and judgments against the business, the proprietor's business and personal assets are subject to liens until the action is satisfied. There may be other advantages and disadvantages as well, but the ones I have identified are the more common ones.

As a tax auditor for the Georgia Department of Revenue, I had to initiate liens and attachments on sole proprietors' businesses and personal assets for failure to pay delinquent sales taxes and employer withholding taxes. This was not something I was proud of or got gratification from; it was simply one of the responsibilities of my job. Proprietors can avoid these kinds of actions by paying these taxes on time or making arrangements with the governing authorities. Proprietors *must* comply with these agreements.

Partnership

A partnership is when individuals, entities (companies), or a combination of both decide to come together and do business, sharing the same interest. Partnerships are often formed when there is a need for special skills or the need to pool or combine capital (funding). There are more reasons why partnerships are formed, but these are two of the main reasons. Different states have created other types of partnerships, but in this book the focus will remain on a general partnership in which all partners share in profits and are responsible for all liabilities.

I highly recommend that, for this type of business, a partnership agreement be executed. This agreement will clearly identify how profits and losses will be distributed; the initial capital invested by the partners; the limit that a partner can obligate the business; and other specifics. The intent of this agreement is to get buy-in from all partners regarding how the business will be operated and to clearly spell out each partner's interest and responsibility. I have always recommended to my partnership clients that they develop a written partnership agreement and have it signed by all partners. One key reason is that I want to make sure that all partners understand what their responsibilities are in operating the business. I have always stated that, even if I were in a partnership with my mother or father, I would still execute an agreement. Family and friendship are great, but when it comes down to business, it's important to act as if you are in business.

A partnership offers the following advantages:

1. the pooling of capital,
2. the pooling of skills,
3. the sharing of liability and responsibility,
4. the ability to grow faster, and
5. the pass-through of profits and losses to partner's individual tax returns, which eliminates income tax on the partnership.

The disadvantages of a partnership include the following:

1. self-employment taxes on partners' shares of profits;
2. disagreements among the partners which can cause the decline of the partnership's effectiveness;
3. unlimited liability (all partners are responsible for debts of the partnership, and their personal assets may be subject to liens and attachments); and
4. each partner's responsibility for the actions of the other partners.

<u>Corporation</u>

A corporation is a separate legal entity created by a state; the state issues a corporate charter that recognizes this legal entity to do business in that state. Corporations are allowed to do business in other states but need to register and follow the respective states' regulations. For the sake of this section, I am limiting my discussion to non-public C corporations.

The main characteristics of a corporation are limited liability and unlimited life. *Limited liability* means that most debts and actions by the officers of the corporation are against the corporation only—not the individuals themselves; in most incidents, officers and shareholders are not personally liable for derogatory actions. Individuals and entities form corporations to raise capital for operation, expansion, and limited liability. Unlimited life in a corporation means when a shareholder dies, sells stock or no longer has interest in the business, the corporation continues to operate until it is dissolved. Corporations raise funds by selling their common shares (stocks) to potential investors.

Forming a corporation offers a number of advantages:

1. limited liability,
2. avoidance of self employment taxes from pass-through profits,
3. unlimited life or perpetual lifetime, and

4. shareholders have the right to vote and receive dividends.

The disadvantages of a corporation include the following:

1. paying income taxes on profits at a higher corporate rate,
2. the high costs required to organize,
3. close scrutiny by the state and the Internal Revenue Service, and
4. creditors' first right to assets during dissolution.

There are other advantages and disadvantages of organizing as a corporation, but those listed above are the primary ones to consider.

Subchapter S Corporation

The Subchapter S corporation (or simply, S corporation) is for individuals and entities who wish to be covered under the corporate umbrella with limited liability. This type of entity is similar to the partnership, with the pass-through of profits and losses to individual shareholders (owners). An S corporation is established under the laws of a particular state and granted an election by the Internal Revenue Service (IRS). The S corporation has only one class of stock, and ownership is limited to one hundred shareholders.

I have seen individuals incorporate and receive election from the IRS as S corporations when their businesses were small in size and a lot of risks were present. An example would be a physician's practice or any type of business that may be subject to higher risks. Risks involve situations in which there is a great potential of physical harm to people or errors that may affect the business's customers in a big way.

The advantages of an S corporation include these:

1. the pass-through of profits and losses to individual shareholders' personal tax returns,
2. the elimination of double taxation (an S corporation does not pay corporate income taxes),
3. relative ease of dissolving (as compared to a C corporation), and
4. shareholders' ability to take nondeductible and nontaxable distributions on a regular basis.

Among the disadvantages are the following:

1. the high costs of establishing an S corporation,
2. close scrutiny by the IRS, and
3. the limited number of shareholders.

There are other advantages and disadvantages to establishing an S corporation; however, the main ones are listed above.

My experience has revealed that S corporations that have regular monthly financial reporting (profit and loss statements, and so on) fare better than the ones that do not. Let me explain. If S corporation shareholders are monitoring their net operating results on a monthly basis, the company can make adjustments to ensure that its pass-through profits do not have an unfavorable result on the shareholders' personal income tax returns. If a business is not monitoring closely or making appropriate adjustments, the pass-through profits to the shareholders' personal income tax returns may put the shareholders in a higher tax bracket than the corporate tax rate on a C corporation.

I once had a physician client whose net profits were consistently very good on a monthly basis. In December of each year, I recommended that she increase her pay or give herself a bonus. The amount of the increase was subject to federal, state, Medicare, and Social Security taxes, but the salary and payroll expenses were considered expenses for the corporation. As a result, the net profit that passed through to her personal income tax return was lower, and her overall income tax liability was lower. I also recommended other ways to reduce her tax liability such as establishing a retirement plan in which the maximum contribution amount could be adjusted from her income.

Limited Liability Corporation (LLC*)*

A limited liability corporation (LLC) is a legal entity that is authorized through the states. Owners of an LLC are called members instead of shareholders. An LLC can consist of a sole individual, a group of individuals, other LLCs, corporations, or foreign entities. Just like the S corporation and partnership, an LLC has a pass-through effect to the members' income tax returns. The cost to organize an LLC is lower than for a Subchapter S corporation or a C corporation. Unlike an S corporation, there is no limit to the number of owners (members).

My experience with LLC members has revealed that they often choose the LLC route because it is fast, easy, and less costly to organize; at the same time, they are under the corporate umbrella with an LLC and have limited liability.

Most of these LLCs are professional companies and small entities that look to expand their operations by adding more investors.

There are a number of advantages to forming an LLC, including:

1. limited liability,
2. lower costs to organize,
3. unlimited number of owners (members),
4. pass-through effect to members' individual income tax returns,

5. no corporate income tax, and
6. management flexibility.

Among the disadvantages are the following:

1. a limit on the types of businesses permitted (banks and insurance companies cannot be LLCs), and
2. the requirement that an LLC that is not classified as a corporation must file an election form with the IRS.

There may be other advantages and disadvantages; however, I listed the main ones above.

I highly recommend that potential business owners understand the different structures and decide which one is best for them. I also recommend that they seek professional advice from an accountant or lawyer.

CHAPTER 2

Do Your Homework

Soon you may find yourself tossing and turning at night, daydreaming, and constantly looking as though something is on your mind. It won't be because you are weird or crazy. And there won't be anything wrong with you either. It's just that your mind will be on that product or service that you dream of providing through your potential business venture.

Prior to starting a business, the entrepreneur *must* prepare himself or herself for this exciting and risky venture. During the preparation stage, entrepreneurs *must* be open-minded, flexible, committed, and honest with customers and themselves.

Research Your Business

The first thing to do is to conduct research of whatever products and services you would like to offer. This research will entail acquiring studies from local and national economic and business entities such as the local chamber of commerce, Small Business

Administration (SBA), and other development centers and resources. These studies will provide you with the demographics of the area, traffic analysis, details regarding the potential need for your products or services, and other valuable information.

The next step is to identify the right location. Location is very important when starting a business. I suggest making frequent visits to your potential location (excluding home-based businesses, of course) to perform your own assessment of the surroundings and the need for your business. For example, if you wanted to open a fast food restaurant that will sell hamburgers, you would probably not consider a location where a McDonald's and Burger King are two to three blocks away. This would be extremely risky regardless of how great your hamburgers are.

I had a client who failed to do his research and opened a restaurant a block away from a nationally known restaurant that sold similar food. During the first two months he realized a constant flow of business until the customers decided to spend their money with his competitor a block away and with other establishments within a one-mile radius. Not long afterward, this client realized a great decline in sales and was forced to lay off employees and close his business. A few months later, he applied all of the lessons he had learned from the first venture and opened another restaurant in a location that was underserved and had less competitors. As a result, his sales increased, and he hired two additional people.

Prepare an Effective Business Plan

Before a business owner starts a business, he or she needs to establish a business plan. The key elements of a business plan include marketing strategies, initial capital, the number and type of employees, the experience of the management team, cash flow analysis, and future-year projections.

The studies mentioned in the research section above are tools that will help entrepreneurs establish effective marketing strategies. If a business owner decides to secure financing from banks, the SBA, or other financial entities, folks at these institutions will want to see his or her marketing plan. The marketing plan should clearly identify the products and/or services the business owner plans to offer and the uniqueness of these products and services. Ask yourself this question: What is unique about my business that my competitors don't have?

An effective business plan should show the experience of the owners and management, and the competence of the employees. I suggest attaching the resumes of the owners, managers, and employees in order to give the banks and financial institutions the sense that these individuals are competent enough to operate the business.

Banks and other financial institutions will want to know your current and future plans; therefore, you may need to prepare a year's cash flow analysis and a five-year projection. The cash flow analysis should show the anticipated inflows versus the anticipated outlays, which will hopefully produce a positive cash flow to service the business's debt and sustain the business. The five-year projection shows the loan officers or investors where you plan to be in five years. Your five-year projection figures should take into account inflation and new strategies for increasing revenue or sales.

Avoid "Idea Killers" (aka "Haters")

Like other things in your life that you are excited about and proud of, you may want to share information about your business venture with others. But, just as there are negative people in your personal life, the same types exist when you are starting or operating a business. I call these negative people "idea killers" or "haters." I define idea killers and haters as people who decide not to encourage you but instead find ways to tell you why you cannot achieve your goal of operating a business.

Let's say that, after you have done your research and prepared an effective business plan, you are convinced that it is a go. Now, you try to share your excitement with a friend or with family members, but you become discouraged based on their comments about or assessments of your plans. These negative individuals may be jealous, unmotivated, uninformed, or all of the above. My recommendation for dealing with idea killers and haters is to keep your business to yourself! If you have to talk about your plans and goals, I suggest you talk to God!

Sometimes a business owner does need assistance to start his or her business. I can remember a client who did his homework, developed a great business plan, and had a great credit score; on top of that, the bank and the SBA were ready to move on his project. He wanted to open a ten-minute oil change business in a great location. When it came time to close on the loan, my client's older brother talked him out of it. My client called the banker and told him that he had changed his mind and would not be pursuing the business after all.

The banker called me and informed me of my client's decision. I called the client and asked what had gone wrong. He informed me that his older brother, who was going to loan him a portion of the start-up funds, had changed his mind. The reason his older brother gave had nothing to do with the availability of funds—his brother had plenty. The reason he gave my client was that he did not think the business would survive one year. The bank and the SBA, however, were convinced that this would be a great and profitable venture located in a perfect area.

Within three months of my client declining the bank loan, the banker offered the plan to another person. It has been over twenty years since this incident, and the ten-minute oil change business is still operating with the same owner. The business always has a line of cars pulled up out front, waiting for oil changes.

CHAPTER 3

Identify and Secure Financing for Your Business

Make the Best Use of Personal Funds and Business Loans

One of the most challenging things for a new business is finding initial or start-up capital. Currently, banks and other financial institutions have strict rules governing loans for start-up capital. I recommend that you secure start-up capital that will carry your business for at least four months. The start-up capital will include anticipated monthly expenses such as salaries, payroll expenses, rent, utilities, loan payments, supplies, merchandise, equipment, and other overhead and operating expenses. I recommend at least four months because it may take your business at least that long to get established and to realize positive cash flows. With four months of start-up capital, if you do not meet your monthly sales or income projection, you will still have enough to take care of your monthly expenses.

The key to starting and operating a business is access to funds. After you have identified how much start-up capital will be required for operation, equipment, and monthly outlays, you will have to determine how to secure the appropriate funding. Funds may be obtained from many places. A business owner may secure funds from a business loan; loans from family and friends; his or her own savings; local economic stimulus funding; and the SBA. I strongly caution business owners *not* to deplete their personal savings to use in a business. These personal funds may be needed for future emergencies. A client of mine once used his entire savings to start his business because he did not want to have any business loans or debts. After four months of operation, his business declined greatly. Realizing a cash flow problem, he tried to secure a business loan from a bank using his unsecured (debt-free) equipment and furniture. But based on the bank policies, my client was not able to use these depreciated assets to secure the amount of money he needed. Therefore, he was unable to secure the loan—even in spite of his great credit score.

I suggest using "other people's money" before depleting your life savings. Other people's money can come in the form of bank loans, SBA loans, and loans from family and friends.

Check Your Own Credit Score

Prior to submitting your business plan to a
financial institution—at which point, they will check
your credit—I suggest checking your own credit
first. Individuals are entitled to a free annual credit
report from the major three credit bureaus. Secure
copies of these reports and aggressively remove and
explain any derogatory items on the reports. Banks
and financial institutions mainly use a person's FICO
score to determine whether to make a loan to him or
her, regardless of how great the business plan is. Loan
officers and loan boards want to feel comfortable that
the debt will be repaid in a timely fashion before they
take a risk. Unfortunately, recent banking changes
have made it very difficult for business owners to
secure financing to start, expand, or operate their
businesses.

Present Your Business Plan

After you have completed your research, established
an effective business plan, and reviewed your credit
report, it is time to submit your business plan to the
bank or financial institution for funding.

This process can be stressful and time-consuming.
Believe me, banks and other financial institutions
will review everything closely. I suggest you present
yourself in a professional manner when meeting with

the bankers and help them to feel that you are serious and competent about operating your business. Banks make their money on loans and new customers; loaning you money to start up, expand, and sustain your business may result in new and continuous business for them too. If your loan is not approved the first time, ask the banker to give you the reasons and then make the necessary corrections and submit your application again. I encourage you to not give up, especially if you have done your homework and you know deep down in your heart that your business will be successful.

I have prepared numerous business plans for clients and have learned over the years that the ones that were rejected were due to credit issues and the clients not being able to convince bankers that they could operate and run efficient businesses.

Again, if your plan and loan are rejected, do not be discouraged. Make whatever corrections are necessary and try again, even if it is with another financial institution or if you need investors. There are other options you have to realize your dream of operating your own business.

CHAPTER 4

Establish Rapport with Key People

Identify Professionals who Can Help You

An effective business owner establishes rapport with the people who can help him or her. These people include bankers, accountants, lawyers, insurance agents, ministers, and other business owners. A business owner does not possess all the skills, knowledge, and abilities required to operate a successful business. When a business owner lacks bookkeeping skills and is not familiar with the state and federal tax requirements, he or she needs to seek advice and assistance from a competent accountant. The business owner needs to identify a lawyer to advise him or her on current and potential legal issues.

The entrepreneur also needs to go to the bank where the company will do business and meet his or her banker. Once a year, you should take your banker to lunch. Business owners also need to identify reputable insurance agents to ensure that they have the proper insurance to protect themselves and their assets. Often, in addition to the stress from everyday life, business owners experience ups and downs while operating their businesses. I suggest seeking spiritual counseling from your minister if the burden becomes overwhelming. It would be a good idea to take your minister or pastor to lunch or dinner too.

Join and Participate in Business Organizations

There is an old saying that "birds of a feather flock together." This also applies for business owners. To expose your business and get to know others whom you can help and who can help you, I suggest joining local business organizations such as the chamber of commerce and ethnic business organizations.

I served for a number of years on the board of directors with the local chamber of commerce in my southeast Georgia hometown. As a board member, I learned and shared information with others about new, current, and future opportunities in my area. I also attended the monthly networking socials. At these networking events, I met different types of business owners and was able to promote my services. As a result, I was able to secure new clients directly and from referrals. I learned that when others see you involved and attending network events, they develop a sense of confidence in you and a willingness to tell others about you and your products or services. As a business owner, you cannot be shy and keep to yourself if you plan to grow and sustain your operation.

Promote Your Business in the Community

There are many advantages to promoting your business throughout the community. I suggest using churches and other public establishments to advertise your products and services. This promotion can be in the form inexpensive flyers, business cards, and word of mouth. You must also support these organizations, for example, purchasing ads in their publications and attending their events. I know this sound like a lot, but you will need to pick and choose which ones to support and make an effort to show that you and your business are concerned about their success. I have also found that making yourself available as a volunteer and supporter in the community not only enhances your reputation but enhances your business too.

Another way of promoting your business is to seek customers outside your community. I call this "doing business across the tracks." You see, when I was a youth in a small town in southeast Georgia, my family and I lived near the railroad tracks. Back then—and even currently in some places—people were segregated based mostly on their ethnicity and wealth. To me, however, the color that counts is the color of money: green. My experience in business has shown me that you have to attract customers regardless of whom they are or where they live. I used to boast that my customer base was 50 percent black and 50 percent white. I learned that most people are not concern about the color of your skin, but the quality of the service you provide. Customers are looking to spend money where they feel that the owner is competent and charges a reasonable price.

I also encourage business owners to establish rapport with and promote their businesses in the Hispanic and other ethnic communities. These communities are rapidly growing and can utilize your products and services too.

The ultimate goal is to treat all customers with the same level of respect and the same high quality of service.

CHAPTER 5

Manage Your Business

Managing a business is not an easy task. A business owner is confronted with events they have control of and ones they do not. During the economic decline in the United States and the world in the last eight years, several businesses have closed their doors, and many have had to revise their way of operating. Unfortunately, unemployment has increased, so many families have suffered financially. With all of this going on in our great country and world, one might ask, "Why start and operate a business?"

Small businesses account for over 80 percent of jobs in the United States. Therefore, I believe that, if we expect the unemployment rate to decline and the US economy to improve, there has to be more emphasis on creating and sustaining small businesses. I am not a noted economist or expert, but I believe that the more people we have working and paying taxes, the more money will be spent on goods and services. This trend will have a positive ripple effect on our economy and communities.

<u>Stay Current with Technology</u>

As technology rapidly changes in our world, entrepreneurs have to change their ways of doing business. Many of the techniques and processes used ten, fifteen, and twenty years ago won't cut it in today's world. Many of the changes are related to the use of computers, cell phones, BlackBerry phones, and other technological devices. In addition to equipment and devices, there are new and effective ways (such as Facebook, LinkedIn, and company websites) to communicate with customers and improve products and services. Effective business owners need to learn about and use these technologies if they want to remain competitive. Business owners need to always seek process improvement initiatives.

I can remember when I used to prepare income taxes by hand. Over twenty-five years ago, I invested in tax preparation software that not only improved my efficiency but also increased how many customers I had. In the same way, when the electronic filing of income tax returns, and the refund anticipation loan and other bank products came into existence, I had to change my way of doing business and invest in the current technology in order for me to be competitive, maintain my customers, and attract new ones.

Hire and Train Competent Employees

Normally the first people a customer sees when entering your business are your employees. How these employees treat your customers may determine how long you have them as customers. To be an effective business owner, you have to make sure you provide the proper customer service and technical training to these important members of your company. Many experts have said that employees are the most important part of a business. In addition to providing proper training, an effective business owner must treat all employees with respect. When hiring folks to work for you, you must ensure that you attract the best people—those who will enhance your company and help customers retain confidence in you.

I witnessed the repercussions for a client of mine whose workforce was not competent or motivated. This client's business suffered, and his reputation was tarnished. The cause of this decline in reputation and the suffering that resulted from it was the hiring of family members and friends who did not have the proper qualifications for the jobs they were hired to do. In my opinion, the employees were comfortable because of the close relationships they had with the owner, and they felt they did not have to go the extra mile to provide good service to his customers. In addition, these employees did not fear being fired or removed from their positions.

Continuously Market Your Business

To be an effective business owner, you cannot be complacent. You will have to constantly think of ways to improve your business and get the word out about your products and services. Marketing can be very expensive depending on the type of media used. Many small businesses cannot afford to advertise in the newspaper, on television, or on radio stations on a regular basis. Even though these media outlets are very effective, there are other, more inexpensive ways to market your business. Professional-looking flyers, business cards, door hangers, the Internet, and, most of all, word of mouth are great ways to market your business. Effective marketing will bring in new businesses and referrals.

A business can develop websites that enable potential customers to learn more about their products and services for free. In addition, your business website can provide potential customers with information about you and your experience. Flyers and business cards may be distributed within the communities you serve at churches, eating establishments, and other public places.

I knew owners that spent a great deal of money marketing their businesses through major media and then did not have enough money to make payroll. The owners felt that by marketing their business through those media outlets, they would be guaranteed to greatly increase the number of customers they served. Sometimes this is true, but business owners must use good judgment and look for other inexpensive but effective ways to get the word out.

<u>Be Honest with Yourself</u>

The excitement and motivation of operating a profitable business can backfire on a business owner. During the operation of your business, you must be open and honest with yourself and understand your financial limitations. Business owners must make appropriate business decisions when it comes to spending money and dealing with competitors, customers, employees, and the general public.

Some business owners focus mainly on the future and what they anticipate, and they fail to pay attention to the current realities of their individual situations. Let's say a business owner's long-range plans are to open a second business location fifty miles away. He spends a tremendous amount of time and money preparing for the second establishment while neglecting the current operation. As a result, the sales and income at the existing location decline, and the business owner has problems paying the monthly expenses. The appropriate management course of action would be to reverse their focus and put all their efforts into improving the current operation in order to sustain it, and then go back to working on the second location.

Being honest with myself has been my greatest weakness. I allow my excitement and motivation to overrule my reality. Instead of focusing on my current situation, I sometimes look to the future and focus on my plans "down the road." I do believe that people should have vision, but at times we have to stop and ensure that our current status and situation are being considered. Not being honest with yourself can put you, your business, and your family in a very stressful situation.

CHAPTER 6

Establish an Effective Recordkeeping System

The major downfalls of many businesses are recordkeeping and not being familiar with the various state and federal laws and regulations. Business owners who lack the required skills and knowledge should hire professionals to assist them. As a tax auditor for the Georgia Department of Revenue, I found that many businesses' financial records were inadequate or absent; and bad recordkeeping had negative effects on these businesses.

Acquire a General Knowledge of Regulations

I am not suggesting that business owners become experts in the laws and regulations that govern their operations, but they do need to have a general knowledge of what is required by the city, county, state, and federal governments. I suggest hiring professionals (such as a lawyer and accountant) to help ensure that you are in full compliance. Business owners can also do their own research and contact the various governing bodies to learn what their responsibilities are.

If I could, I would tell business owners one key point related to this issue: *All the money that comes into your cash registers or bank accounts from goods and services is not your money!* What I mean is that some of the funds you generate from your operation have to go to various government entities. In other words, you are acting as an agent for these government entities. For example, if you have a retail business in which you collect sales taxes, the sales taxes belong to the states in which you live and where you do business. The state distributes a portion of the sales taxes to your local governments. You are required to pay your rent, utilities, payroll, payroll expenses, and other overhead and operating expenses out of the funds that come in your business. Whatever is left after that is your money.

For eight years, my job was collecting delinquent sales, withholding, and corporate taxes for the State of Georgia. I have experience collecting from small companies and large corporations. One of the largest cases I was involved with had to do with the delinquency of sales and withholding taxes due from a company that operated a riverboat. This company failed to pay their sales and withholding taxes for six months. As a result, judgments and liens were placed on the company's assets including bank accounts, inventory, and the riverboat. Because the company did not comply with the established payment agreement, *the riverboat and other company assets were seized by the State of Georgia.* Naturally, news of this event was in the media for over a month, until the liability was satisfied and the riverboat was purchased by a new set of investors. This is an example of the worst that can happen when business owners neglect their legal responsibilities.

Acquire a General Knowledge of Financial Reporting

Again, I am not suggesting that business owners must be accountants or financial experts. However, a business owner should be able to read and understand the various financial reports produced by his or her accountant or accounting software. These reports may consist of a balance sheet, income statement (profit and loss), and statement of cash flow. The balance sheet gives the financial position of the business at a given time, usually at the end of the month. The balance sheet consists of assets, liabilities, and equity (net worth) sections. The income statement shows the income versus expenses and gives the net result of operation—whether a net income (profit) or loss (deficit). The statement of cash flow identifies the cash generated and its uses for a specified period, usually a given month or the same period as the balance sheet and income statement. The statement of cash flow also shows the cash activity relating to operating activities, investing activities, financing activities, and supplemental information. To learn more detail about these financial reports, please review accounting books and other accounting resources.

For effective financial reporting and accuracy, I suggest that a business owner invest in one of the numerous accounting software programs. It is *imperative* that, before you begin entering data in your software, you make sure that the charts of accounts are properly set up. Seek professional help if you need to. I have had clients who decided to do their own monthly bookkeeping and accounting using software packages. These clients then brought me flash drives or back up disks and printouts of their year-end financial operations. I then had to make numerous adjustments in order to prepare their annual business or corporate returns. Their errors included things like having a liability account set up as an expense, which then overstated or understated their year-end results.

A business owner should feel so confident about their financial records that they would welcome governing agencies such as the IRS and state and local governments to review or audit their books.

CHAPTER 7

The Effective Community Economic Model

I believe that, as human beings, we have a responsibility to serve our communities. Furthermore, I also believe that business owners should serve and be visible in their communities. This is not just a responsibility—it makes good business sense too. Business owners should do their best to enhance the economic conditions in their communities.

This section of the book not only addresses the responsibilities of business owners, but it also challenges other established community organizations such as our churches and civic and social organizations to play active roles in promoting the economy in their communities.

Pooling of Financial Resources

Often, due to limited financial resources, communities may find it difficult to initiate projects that would greatly benefit their area. Therefore, it might take businesses, organizations, or a combination of both to start and execute these projects. An advantage of this pooling is that there will be more leveraging; financial institutions may be more willing to loan money when they know there is more than one entity at risk. Disadvantages might be in-fighting, turf wars, envy, and problems deciding who should lead. Unfortunately, the disadvantages seem to take priority over the advantages and benefits of many of these projects.

I once had the opportunity to provide services to three investment groups. These investment groups started off with eight to twelve investors apiece. The goal of two of the investment groups was to purchase old houses, fix them up, and sell them for a profit. The other investment group's main initial focus was to profit from stock investments; however, their long-range goal was to develop multifamily housing and rent units out to the public. There were numerous disagreements relating to the original goals in all three of the groups. Two groups ceased operating after five years. The third investment group ceased after eight years; and the group's two goals had changed to just one: investing in the stock market.

In order to create an effective operation, all who pool their resources must be on the same page and support the organization's goal. They must realize that it may take a while to receive returns on their investments. I feel that the participants who are pooling their resources must not only focus on the short-term goals and benefits but also on the long-term goals and benefits. The benefits I am referring to may be tangible and intangible ones that will benefit the overall community and the investors. The benefits are addressed in the following sections.

<u>Community Benefits</u>

Whether business owners and organizations come together or operate solely, the community can benefit in many ways. As previously stated, over 80 percent of jobs in the United States are created by small businesses. Going forward, the establishment of new businesses and joint ventures will greatly help decrease the unemployment rates in our communities. Joint or sole business ventures restore trust and confidence among the people, particularly our youth. Economic prosperity in our communities will help decrease crime, financial hardships on families, and even homelessness.

<u>The Effective Model</u>

Joint-venture projects in the community may involve businesses and organizations. For the sake of this book, I chose for my model one of the most respectable and visible organizations in the community, the church. This model depicts the pooling of resources and the resulting enhancement of the economic environment in a community. In an effective community economic model, *the dollar will turn over several times.*

The chosen model identifies seven churches in the community that are pooling their resources and establishing a tax-exempt 501(c)(3) community development corporation (CDC). The main purpose of the CDC is to create jobs, business opportunities, housing, and other goodwill initiatives in the community.

THE EFFECTIVE COMMUNITY
ECONOMIC MODEL

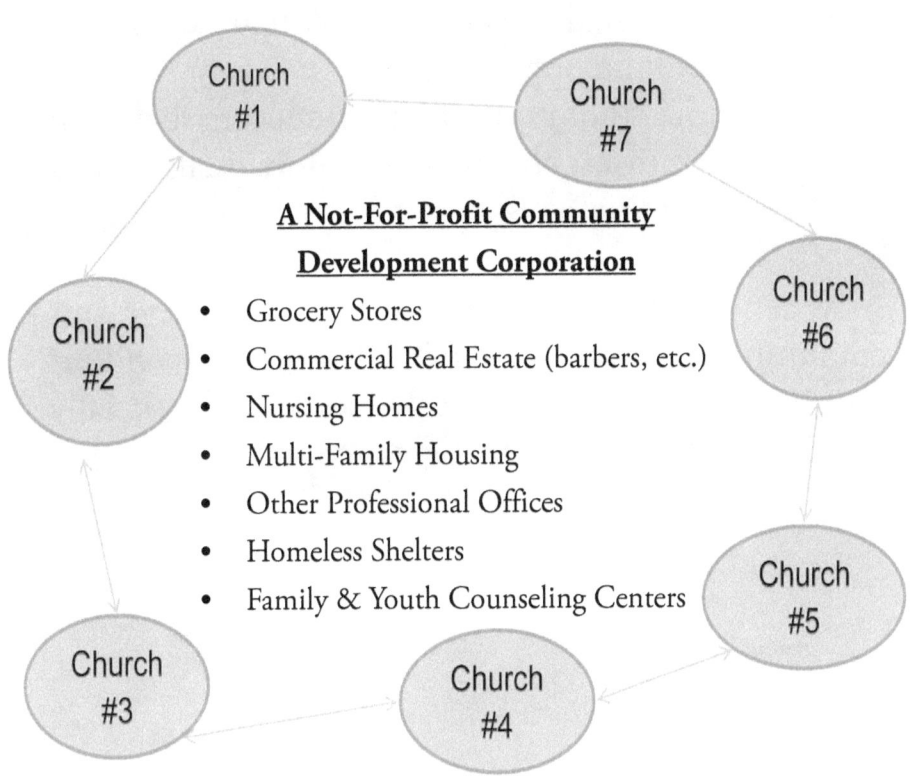

Church #1

Church #7

A Not-For-Profit Community Development Corporation

- Grocery Stores
- Commercial Real Estate (barbers, etc.)
- Nursing Homes
- Multi-Family Housing
- Other Professional Offices
- Homeless Shelters
- Family & Youth Counseling Centers

Church #2

Church #6

Church #3

Church #4

Church #5

As a visionary and strong advocate for small businesses, I truly believe we as Americans can help solve our unemployment and economic conditions in our country. We must do the following:

- actively encourage entrepreneurship
- support small businesses through legislation and banking opportunities
- promote the pooling of resources between organizations, businesses, individuals, or a combination of all

When we perform these actions, I believe our communities, towns, and cities will realize tremendous economic growth and help solve some of the socially and economic issues in this great country of ours!!

www.ingramcontent.com/pod-product-compliance
Lightning Source LLC
Chambersburg PA
CBHW021925170526
45157CB00005B/2195